The Man from the Sky

Julian Thomlinson

D0584507

Series Editors:
Rob Waring and Sue Leather
Series Story Consultant: Julian Thomlinson
Story Editor: Sue Leather

NATIONAL GEOGRAPHIC LEARNING | CENGAGE Learning

Australia • Brazil • Japan • Korea • Mexico • Singapore • Spain • United Kingdom • United States

Page Turners Reading Library

The Man from the Sky

Julian Thomlinson

Publisher: Andrew Robinson

Executive Editor: Sean Bermingham

Editorial Assistant: Dylan Mitchell

Director of Global Marketing:
Ian Martin

Senior Content Project Manager:
Tan Jin Hock

Manufacturing Planner:
Mary Beth Hennebury

Contributors:
Vessela Gasper, Jessie Chew

Layout Design and Illustrations:
Redbean Design Pte Ltd

Cover Illustration: Eric Foenander

ISBN-13: 978-1-4240-4651-5

ISBN-10: 1-4240-4651-3

National Geographic Learning
20 Channel Center Street
Boston, Massachusetts 02210
USA

Cengage Learning is a leading provider of customized learning solutions with office locations around the globe, including Singapore, the United Kingdom, Australia, Mexico, Brazil, and Japan. Locate your local office at:
international.cengage.com/region

Cengage Learning products are represented in Canada by Nelson Education, Ltd.

Visit National Geographic Learning online at
NGL.Cengage.com

Visit our corporate website at
www.cengage.com

Printed in the United States of America
1 2 3 4 5 6 7 – 18 17 16 15 14

Contents

Review

Background Reading

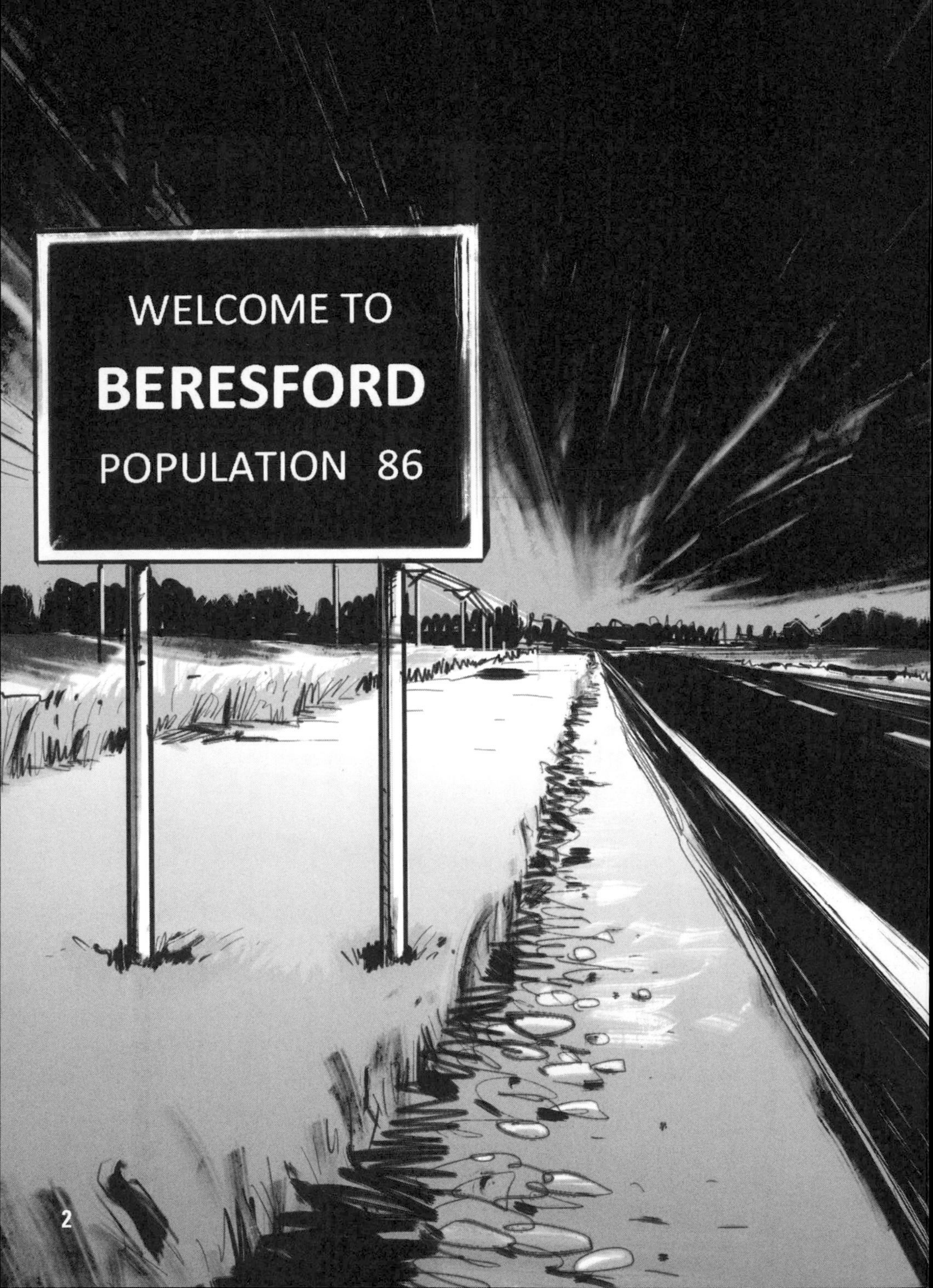
WELCOME TO
BERESFORD
POPULATION 86

People in the story

Beth Fowler
a young woman who takes
care of her sick father

Noel Fowler
Beth's father, who has
multiple sclerosis

Elise Kendall
a government agent

Roger Stone
a government agent

Lael
a mysterious stranger

The story is set in the Minnesota countryside, USA.

Chapter 1

The light in the sky

Beth woke up with her heart beating like crazy. What was that *noise*? She'd gone to bed after a really bad night with her father and was dreaming about a boy she knew in high school. The next thing she knew there was this great sound, this BOOM, and she was sitting up in bed in a cold sweat. It had been a noise like a car crashing into her front door. Maybe there was someone at the door? Who would beat on her front door in the middle of the night?

At first she didn't want to move—she was too scared. What if it was some kind of crazy man? Had she even locked the door? It wasn't like the city out here. Out here in Beresford, Minnesota, population 86, people didn't worry so much about locking doors. Beresford was the kind of place where everybody knew everybody else and helped each other and nothing crazy ever happened to anybody. Except now it sounded like something had exploded just outside her house.

Silly girl, Beth thought to herself. *There might be somebody out there who needs your help.* She got out of bed, pulled on a T-shirt and hurried down the stairs, wiping the sleep from her eyes. She hoped her father was still asleep or he'd be scared and confused. Had she dreamed the noise? She didn't think she had. If she had dreamed it she'd feel silly standing about in her nightclothes. It was still summer but there was a coldness in the air. She ran her fingers through her hair and opened the door.

There was nobody there. There was nobody there but she

could smell smoke and something else. Something . . . strange. It was like oranges and . . . something else. But what? She'd never smelled anything like it in her life. She listened carefully but couldn't hear anything except that dog, and wondered whose it was. There was nothing to see—it was a dark night and the only light was the one from inside her house. She thought she'd better take a look around so she got a light from the kitchen and went outside. The moment she opened the door a blue-pink light came out of the forest, shooting up from the trees with a WHOOSH and sending a wave of heat that knocked her off her feet.

What was *that*?! Her first thought was her father, so she hurried back inside to check on him. He was lying in his bed—somehow he'd managed to throw the covers off himself—and he was staring at her with wide, terrified eyes.

"Shh, Daddy," she said. "It's OK. It's OK." She didn't know what else to say to him because she didn't know what had happened herself. Her own heart was beating hard. Her father's mouth was moving as if he wanted to say something, but he couldn't, and she knew it must be driving him crazy. More than anything else in the world, she wished she knew what he was thinking, what he wanted to say. All she could say was sorry—that was all she could ever say. It seemed like a day couldn't go by without having to say sorry, and sometimes it made her angry. When she got angry, she remembered one thing he had once told her, before he had gotten really sick. He had told her that whatever happened, she should always know that he loved her—that would be true no matter what. So she thought about that now as she held his hand and told him she'd have to leave him for a little while to make sure there was nobody outside that needed her help.

Her hands were still shaking when she went downstairs, still shaking when she picked up the telephone. She felt she ought to call somebody. But whom? Ted Rosier over at the police station? What would she say to him? That she'd smelled something funny and seen a light in the sky? She could imagine what Ted Rosier would say to that—probably he'd smile and ask her if she'd been drinking again. Maybe there would be something on the radio, she thought, but when she tried to turn it on it didn't work at all. The TV was the same—she couldn't even get a picture. The coffee machine worked fine at least, so she made herself a cup of coffee and sat with it on the sofa, her knees pulled up to her chest. She was sitting like that, wishing it were daylight when things could get back to normal, when someone knocked on her front door.

She shouted out in surprise and almost dropped the coffee all over herself. Thinking it was maybe Bonnie or Dave Walker from the house down the road, she got up and opened the door and got the biggest shock she'd ever had in her twenty-eight years of life on the planet Earth.

Outside stood a man—a tall man with eyes so blue they were almost purple. That wasn't the strangest thing about him though. The strangest thing was that he wasn't wearing any clothes. She checked again: no, he wasn't wearing any clothes at all.

Beth opened her mouth to speak but no sound came out. Instead it was the man who spoke, in the most polite voice Beth had ever heard.

"Excuse me," he said. "If it wouldn't be too much trouble, I'd be very pleased if you could offer me some help."

Then he fell down and didn't move.

Chapter 2

The visitor

For a moment Beth just stood and looked at him. The man still hadn't moved. She ran inside and picked up the phone to call the hospital, but it didn't work. There was no sound coming out of it at all. It was the same with her cell phone. She could feel herself starting to panic but she pushed it back down and checked on the man. She didn't even know if he was still alive, so she sat down on the floor next to him. She had to touch him to check that he was still alive, but it didn't feel right, with him not wearing clothes and all. Telling herself she had no choice, she put a hand on him.

He was so cold! Was he dead? No—she could feel his heart. It was so fast—a hundred beats per minute at least. Why was he so cold? *What do you expect, girl?* she said to herself. *He's not wearing any clothes.* She had to get him to a doctor, she thought, and wondered how she could do it. She tried to lift him and felt a sharp pain shoot up her back. Bad idea. There was no way she'd get him into her car. He'd fallen down sideways and was lying across the front of her doorway. Maybe she could get him inside—when the phones started working again she could call for help. Should she cover him up first? What if he were dangerous? She pushed these thoughts out of her mind—it was thinking like that that made the world as bad as it was. *If only Daddy could help,* she thought, then realized maybe it was a good thing he wasn't going to find a man who wasn't wearing any clothes outside his front door.

The best thing she could do was get him in the house. First she went back inside and got an old coat. She covered his body and tried again, pulling him inside by the legs, and saying a silent sorry as his head hit the edge of the door. By the time she got him into the living room, she was covered in sweat. She tried to make him comfortable on the floor, and then fell down on a chair by the window. Who was he? Did he have something to do with the noise and the strange light? She wondered if he'd been hurt and lost his mind as well as his clothes. She hoped he was all right. She studied his face. It was easy to like, all right. Not exactly handsome, but . . . good. It was a good face.

She tried the phone again: nothing. She wondered what she might do but couldn't think of anything, so she lay down on the sofa. I'll just close my eyes a moment, she thought. *I won't sleep*, she told herself, *I won't go to sleep*, but she did.

◇◇◇

The first shock of the day came as soon as Beth opened her eyes. The man was sitting cross-legged on the floor in front of her with the coat lying next to him. He still wasn't wearing any clothes.

"Could you . . ." Beth said, pointing at the coat.

"Could I what?" he asked, very politely. He didn't seem to understand, so Beth took the coat and laid it over him, looking the other way as she did so.

"Thank you," he said. Again Beth found she didn't know what to do.

"I expect you have many questions," the man said. Suddenly his calm face made her angry.

"Yes, I sure do," she said, getting up. "To begin with, who are you and what are you doing here? I thought you were dying or something. I hurt my back bringing you in here! And why aren't you wearing any clothes?"

"I will be very happy to answer any and all of your questions . . . ," he said.

Any and all of your questions, Beth thought, *who is this guy?*

". . . but first I must ask you to help me once more."

"Help you?" Beth said. "Now wait a minute."

"Very soon some people will arrive at your door. They are looking for me." Beth felt frightened suddenly. "I must ask you to tell them I am not here. Tell them you have not seen me."

"And if I don't?"

"I am not forcing you," the man said. "I am asking; that is all."

"Who are these men? Police?"

"I believe they are agents of your government," the man said. Beth stood up and started toward the door.

"Sure, I'll help you," she said quickly. The man shook his head.

"I can see you are lying," he said. "That's all right. I understand you are scared. But you have no reason to be scared of me. You really don't."

"Why are agents of the government looking for you?" Beth asked.

"I can't tell you," he said simply.

"Get out of here. Now," Beth said.

"I can't tell you because you won't believe me."

"I said get out."

"Listen to me please," he began. "You live here with your father who is very sick. You've been looking after him since your mother died. He was sick before but he's become much worse since then and even though you love him you wish you could get away, as far away from him as possible."

"Now wait a minute," Beth said.

"I am sorry but I must continue. It's like you live only to care for your father but now he can't even move or speak and you sometimes wish that he weren't here anymore, that you could just get away and leave this place forever. You feel very bad about this and sometimes cry about it at night and tell yourself that maybe tomorrow he'll be better; maybe you'll be able to talk to him. You wish that more than anything, that you could just talk to him. You are so lonely."

"Stop it!" Beth said. There were tears in her eyes.

"My name is Lael," he said. "Please help me now."

Before she could answer, there was a knock at the door.

Chapter 3

Government business

There were two of them, a man and a woman. Both were taller than she and both wore smart clothes. To Beth they looked more like businesspeople than government agents. The man was a little older and wore a hat and sunglasses. She asked them who they were as she looked out at them from behind the door.

"Ma'am, my name is Agent Elise Kendall and this is Agent Roger Stone," she said. "We're with the National Security Agency. Might we ask you a few questions?"

The woman held out her ID card. Beth read "US Government" next to the woman's name.

"What about?" she said.

"It's nothing to worry about," said Agent Elise Kendall, smiling. She had beautiful teeth. "May we come in?"

Beth was about to open the door but then she thought about what the man in her living room had said to her. Whatever happened, she needed to know how he knew what he knew. So instead she stepped outside, closing the front door behind her and moving the two agents backwards.

"We can talk out here," Beth said. "My father's sick and I don't want to worry him."

"Oh, I'm so sorry," said Agent Kendall, but she didn't look all that sorry to Beth.

Agent Stone still hadn't said anything, and he still hadn't taken off his hat or sunglasses. Beth didn't like that either. Now he was putting his hand to his ear. *Why is he doing that?*, Beth wondered, and then she saw he was wearing an earpiece. *This is like a movie*, she thought.

"So what can I do for you?" she asked.

"Miss Fowler . . . you are Miss Beth Fowler?"

Beth nodded.

"Miss Fowler, did you notice anything strange last night?"

"I sure did," she said. Beth told them about the noise waking her up, the light in the sky, and her phone and the lights not working. She stopped before she said anything about the man in her house.

"And what did you do?" Agent Kendall asked her.

"I tried to call the police to find out what was happening but as I said the phones weren't working."

"And you didn't see anyone?" Kendall asked, happily. Beth knew she should say something but she found, much to her surprise, that she didn't want to. There was something about these two—Agent Kendall with her perfect teeth and Agent Stone with his hat still on and his hand on his ear—that she didn't like much. Hoping she wasn't making the biggest mistake of her life, she said, "No. Like I said, the lights were all out anyway. But I'm sure there was nobody around. This is the middle of nowhere, as you may have noticed."

"Miss Fowler, we're looking for someone." This was Agent Stone. Beth was surprised by how soft his voice was. "We believe they are dangerous." Beth thought of the man in her front room. *He didn't seem dangerous, but how did she know?*

"Dangerous?" Beth asked. "Can you tell me what they look like?"

"No, not at this time," Agent Kendall said.

"You're saying 'they.' Is it a man or a woman?"

"We aren't sure," Kendall explained.

"I see," said Beth. "So if you don't know who they are, why do you think they might be dangerous?"

Kendall and Stone looked at each other before answering.

"That's government business," said Stone.

"Government business," said Beth. The two agents looked at one another again. Each of them hoped the other would speak.

"I know it must sound very strange," said Kendall. "The important thing is that you must let us know immediately if you see anybody strange in the area. Can I ask you to do that?"

"Of course," Beth said. Agent Kendall gave her a name card. Beth pretended to look at it then put it in her pocket. She watched as the two agents walked back to their car and drove off, then went back inside.

The man who called himself Lael was still sitting in her living room. He looked like he hadn't moved and he still had the coat over him.

"Thank you," he said simply.

"OK," Beth said. "OK. I got those two out of here but I want you to tell me who you are and how you know about me. If you don't, I'm going to pick up the phone and call this agent and tell them to come and get you and take you away."

"I'm a visitor from another world," he said.

Beth just stood and looked at him. She hadn't expected that answer.

"OK," she said. She took her phone and Kendall's name card out of her pocket.

"It's true," Lael said.

"I must be so stupid," Beth said, putting in the number. "The front door's open—you can get out and start—"

She didn't finish her sentence. The phone dropped from her hand and her mouth fell open. She couldn't possibly be looking at what she was looking at.

In front of her on the floor, instead of a man with a coat over him, was a purple crystal about half a meter tall. Its surface was like diamond, but it was moving like the surface of water, as if it were alive.

Beth screamed.

Chapter 4

Crystal

Beth felt sick just looking at it. The little crystal made a strange sound—the closest thing she could think of was a music box. Her legs felt like water and she thought she might fall but then the air moved in front of her— everything seemed to move just a little bit—and instead of the purple crystal, Lael was back in front of her, holding her arm to stop her from falling.

"I'm going to be sick," Beth said.

"I was telling you there was nothing to be afraid of," said Lael, "but I see now you were unable to understand me in my other form."

He helped her onto the sofa. A couple of minutes passed before she could speak again. She had just seen something impossible, and it felt as though it couldn't fit in her mind, like her head was going to explode. She just couldn't take it all in: the lights in the sky, the strange man, the government agents, and now this.

"What is this?" she finally said. "Is this some kind of trick? Is it a joke? If it's a joke it's not funny. At all! Who are you?"

"I have already answered this question."

"What were you doing at my door with no clothes on?"

"I was injured from my crash and low on energy. I used the last of it to go into a human shape so you would help me. Then I went into a sleep state."

Beth thought about how cold he had been, and that strange heartbeat she had felt.

"Oh, my," was all she could say. "Oh my oh my oh my."

"I traveled here from my home in what you call the Beta Lyrae System. It's about 900 million light years away."

"Could you just . . . stop talking for a moment?" Beth said.

She went into the bathroom and put cold water over her face. Unless she had completely lost her mind there was an alien in her living room. *Maybe I have lost my mind*, she thought. Maybe that's what happens when you have to live in a town of 86 people and spend your life taking care of someone who can't move or talk or do much at all. She looked back into the living room. Still there. Beth thought there was a good chance she had lost her mind, but decided that she had to pretend everything was normal, that she really did have a visitor from outer space in her living room. At least until the doctors came to take her away.

"I'm going to get you some clothes to wear," she said.

"I'm quite warm enough," Lael said, standing up with his arms out wide. "And besides, I have something to show you."

"You've shown me quite enough, thanks," Beth said.

◇◇◇

After she had managed to get Lael dressed, he insisted that she go with him out to the forest to check on his ship. Somehow he managed to get her to agree to go with him. Before they left she had checked the road for the agents, but it seemed as though they had gone for now. Then she took a hammer from a cupboard under the stairs and put it down the back of her jeans: friendly purple alien or not, she didn't trust him at all.

"You haven't told me how you knew what I was thinking about," Beth said, breathing hard.

"My . . . people . . . speak using their minds. We don't have language like you. I have learned to read human thoughts."

"Oh, yeah?" said Beth. "You can read minds? What am I thinking now?"

"It's not clear," Lael explained. "Your brain is messy and confused." *He was right there,* Beth thought. "You are carrying that hammer because you are worried about what I might do."

"You don't need to read thoughts to know that," she said. "What number am I thinking of?"

"Thirty-seven," Lael said after a moment. He was right.

Well, Beth thought, *if that's a trick, it's a good one.*

"Here we are," Lael said.

They stepped out of the trees into a clearing. At least it looked like a clearing, but now Beth got a good look at it she could see that it wasn't. It was a perfect circle; beneath her feet the trees were completely flat and burned black. It was as if someone had dropped a big burning wheel from the sky.

"What is this?" she said.

"Please be calm," Lael told her and raised his arm. Just like in her living room, the air seemed to move, and then what looked like a big purple crystal ball appeared in the sky in front of her.

"What is that?" Beth asked.

"This is my ship," Lael said. He held both hands up toward it and closed his eyes. "It's worse than I thought."

What's worse? Beth thought. She wished she could say something intelligent but it was getting harder all the time.

"The damage," he said. "My ship was badly damaged in the crash. I need to repair it before they find me."

"Who? These government agents?"

"That's right. I am not the first visitor from our world. Some years ago my . . . brothers . . . tried to begin relations with your people. But they went missing. I came here to find them, but something happened as I landed. Oh, no."

"What's the problem?" Beth asked.

"The crystal store is too low. I can't repair it."

Beth was going to ask what that meant but another noise stopped her. She listened carefully.

"What is it?" Lael asked.

"A helicopter," Beth said. "We'd better get out of here."

Chapter 5

Being human

By the time they got back to the house, Beth was scared. The black car was back at the end of her road and they had to go around the side of the house so the agents wouldn't see them. Then there were the helicopters. There were three of them now, circling over the woods. She thought about movies she had seen, ones where soldiers always came in big trucks and took everybody away. She was scared and she found she was getting angry with Lael for making her scared. It was past her father's breakfast time, so she went into the kitchen to make him some eggs and try and calm herself down. Lael followed behind her.

"I must find a supply of silicon in order to repair my ship," he was saying. "A very large supply. Sand might do, although sand is not a pure source. Making it pure would take time. Quartz would be better."

"Quartz," said Beth.

"Quartz, yes," he said. "Do you know where I can find quartz?"

"Can you wait a minute?" Beth said. "I need to make breakfast."

"It's very important," Lael replied. Beth wanted to get him to wait but she knew it would do no good. Instead she switched off the cooker, opened up her computer, and did an Internet search.

"There's an old quarry over in Olmsted County, about two hours' drive away," she said.

"We must go now!" Lael said, moving toward the door.

"Wait a second," Beth said.

"What? Please. You must help me!" he said. It was strange—his voice and face were calm but Beth knew he was in a panic.

"If we go out there those two agents are going to see us," Beth said.

Lael looked out of the corner of the window.

"Oh, I see," he said.

"We can wait until this evening, can't we? I can take you when it gets dark."

Lael looked uncertain.

"If we go now the workers will be there anyway. At the quarry, I mean. You won't be able to do anything until they've gone." Beth realized she was going to be helping an alien steal an important public resource, but she decided she couldn't think about that now.

"I will wait, then," Lael said.

"Good," Beth told him. "Now if you don't mind, I need to make breakfast for my father."

"I'm sorry," Lael said. "Can I help?"

Beth shook her head.

"Do you mind if I ask what's wrong with him?" Lael asked.

"It's called multiple sclerosis," Beth said. "It's very advanced now. It used to be that he would get sick for a time, and he couldn't speak or move properly, then he'd get better and be almost normal. But he's been like this since Momma died. You don't think you could help him, do you?"

Lael shook his head. "I'm sorry. I . . . we . . . don't have a very good knowledge of the human body. It would be impossible. May I meet him?" Lael asked, pointing up at her father's room.

Beth thought about it and then had an idea.

"Could you communicate with him?" Beth asked. "I mean, using your mind?"

"Does the sickness affect his brain?" Lael asked.

"No," Beth explained. "That's the thing about it. His mind is perfectly normal. It's just in a body that doesn't work."

"I can try," Lael said.

◇◇◇

When they went upstairs her father was still awake, but he looked calmer, even when Lael walked into the room. That was a good sign.

"Daddy, you must have a lot of questions about the noise and what's been going on," Beth began, "but first there's someone I want you to meet. Daddy, this is Lael. Lael, this is my father, Noel Fowler."

"It's a pleasure to meet you, sir," said Lael, taking her father's hand.

"Daddy, I want you to relax now," Beth went on. "Lael is . . . he has a kind of gift, Daddy. He wants to help us. I can't really explain—you'll have to see for yourself."

She could see the worry appear in her father's eyes but there was no use trying to explain he was about to have his mind read by an alien. Instead she nodded to Lael, who took her father's hand and looked at him carefully. After a moment, he spoke.

"He's scared," Lael said. "He wants to know what's going on. He wants to know who I am. He can feel what I'm doing and he's confused."

"Daddy, Lael has a very special gift," Beth said. "You can trust him."

"That's better," Lael said. "Beth, I'm going to speak out loud so it's clear to you. Mr. Fowler, I can understand your thoughts. Right now you are thinking this is one of the most frightening, but also the most amazing, things you have ever experienced. Now you're thinking my eyes are a strange purple color; now you're thinking how . . . how can I know these things? The important thing is I do know them and now you have a chance to speak to your daughter."

A tear rolled down her father's face, and Beth, holding his other hand, began to cry.

"Daddy?" she said. "Daddy, can you hear me?"

"I hear you," Lael said, although there was something different in his voice. Then she understood why: Lael was speaking her father's thoughts.

"Daddy . . ." Beth said. After wanting to talk to her father for so long, suddenly she didn't know what to say.

"I'm sorry, Beth," Lael said. "For all of this. For all this."

"Don't say that," Beth replied. "You shouldn't feel bad. I just . . . I just miss you, Daddy. I miss you and I miss Mom."

"I know you do," Lael said. "And I'm so proud of you— how strong you are. I hate this so much, being like this, and the only thing that gets me through it is you. Knowing you're all right. That's what keeps me going. I want to say thank you for that. Thank you so much."

"You don't need to say that," Beth said. "I don't do so much." She suddenly noticed that Lael's hand was very hot—his eyes were closed and sweat had come through his shirt. This is hurting him, she thought, but she couldn't quite manage to end it.

"Daddy, I think we have to go now," Beth said. "I think this is difficult for him."

"One last thing," Lael said. "Who is this . . . man?"

"He's from . . . another place, Daddy."

"I can't," Lael said, in his own voice again. "I'm sorry, I can't."

"Don't apologize," Beth said. She pulled Lael toward her and put her arms around both of the men. "I can never thank you enough for this."

Then a voice spoke in her mind. "You can," it said. "Help him."

She turned to Lael to ask what he meant but then realized it wasn't his voice that she had heard—it was her father's.

Chapter 6

Connections

Lael and her father both slept for the rest of the day. Beth wanted to ask Lael more about what had happened, about hearing her father's voice in her mind, but decided it could wait—now it was her turn to help. She filled the car up with gas, printed out a map to the quarry from her computer, and thought about how to get Lael to it. All day, helicopters flew above her house, and she saw a few big trucks pass down the main road toward the forest. When Lael woke up, she told him about her plan. He laughed, but agreed that it was the best chance they had.

It was dark when she walked out to her car, and Agents Kendall and Stone were still parked beside it. She took her bag off her shoulder as she approached their car.

"Hi there, Agent Kendall," Beth said. "I guess you're still looking for . . . whoever it is you're looking for."

"Until we find them, Miss Fowler," Kendall replied. She noticed Beth's bag. "Going somewhere?" the agent asked.

"Just taking some things back to my friend's place over in Rochester," Beth said. "Why are you still here anyway?"

"For your protection," said Agent Kendall. "We have agents at all the houses in the area."

"Well, thanks, I guess," Beth said, making for her car.

"One thing, Miss Fowler," Agent Kendall said. "You don't want to be too long. We may have to close the whole area off soon and nobody will be able to get in or out."

"Close off the area. Why?" Beth asked. "Let me guess: government business?"

"That's right," she replied.

Beth put her bag on the back seat and started up the engine. She felt the agents' eyes on her as she pulled onto the road and drove off. After a few miles, when she was sure nobody was following her, she said, "OK, you can come out now."

She didn't see quite how he did it, but she heard movement on the back seat and then Lael was sitting there, putting on some of her father's old clothes she had packed in the bag with him.

"Thank you again," he said.

"It might be a good idea to stay low in that seat," Beth said. "You never know who we might pass on the road."

"Right," said Lael, and dropped down out of sight.

She passed by a few cars on the road, and there was one moment when she held her breath as a truck passed her, but mostly the road was quiet, as it was always quiet. She wanted to ask about her father but she was scared Lael might say she had imagined it or something. Instead, she asked about his world, and listened in amazement as he told her about the crystal cities in the sky of his home planet, and about the journeys his people had made across the universe.

"It is easy for us," he told her. "We live a long time so we have a long time to learn."

"Oh, yeah?" Beth said. "How old are you then?"

"I'm not sure I should say," Lael said. "You might feel strange about it."

"Try me," she said.

"I'm a little under six hundred thousand of your Earth years," he told her.

"Six hundred thousand!" Beth said. She couldn't even imagine that long. She thought back to high school science. "Isn't that longer than human beings have existed?"

"It is, yes," Lael admitted.

"Oh," was all she could say. It did make her feel strange. Sad. She would have seventy or eighty years if she was lucky.

"Maybe that is why your feelings are so strong," Lael said, almost to himself. "Because your lives are short you feel everything with such energy. I wish I could experience that."

You're not missing much, believe me, Beth thought.

"I'm not sure about that," said Lael. Beth looked back at him—she kept forgetting he could see into her mind.

"It's amazing how you do that, how you're in my mind like that."

"To me as well," Lael said.

"Even after six hundred thousand years?" she asked.

"It's different," he said.

"What's it like, though?" she asked. "Being inside a human mind?"

"It's . . . beautiful," was all he would say, and Beth couldn't think of a reply.

They drove in silence for a while after that and it wasn't much longer before they passed through Bledsoe and arrived at the old Arrowhead Quarry. She switched off the lights when they got close and drove the car off the road so anyone passing wouldn't see them. When she opened the door to get out, Lael told her to stop.

"Now what?" asked Beth.

"I will do this alone," he said.

"What if you need help?" Beth said.

"You've done enough. You can't take the risk."

She opened her mouth to argue, but then there was a blue light inside her mind and she knew it was no good, that he would not let her. For a moment she almost felt as though she had seen into his mind, and it was like looking at a picture that's too big to see.

"Did I . . . just . . . ?" she asked.

"You did," he said.

"But how?"

"We are making a . . . connection," he said, then he was gone.

Beth watched him run up toward the quarry entrance and disappear into the shadows. She had just seen into his mind, and it was an amazing feeling. She wanted to do it herself. *Be careful*, she thought, trying to reach him, but there was no answer.

Silly girl, she suddenly thought to herself. Why would he be listening out for you? She felt angry with herself for that. *Are you getting feelings for a small, purple crystal? Are there so few good men around here?*

She tried to make herself think about something else and found herself thinking about the time her Daddy had brought her to the quarry when she was a little girl. She remembered how happy he had been with her, as they'd cut a little piece of dark quartz from the rock face and taken it home. She still had it somewhere. She thought of how big and strong her father had seemed, how she could never have imagined him weak and old, and the thought made her get upset. She was thinking that she might cry when she heard a noise on the road that made her jump.

Cars. No, not just cars. Trucks as well. She got out of the car and crept along to the edge of the road. There were at least three of them heading toward her.

Lael, she thought, trying to send her thoughts out to him. *Somebody is coming!*

But there was no reply. Without thinking about it she began running up the edge of the road toward the quarry.

Chapter 7

The quarry

Beth ran up the side of the road, breathing hard. She could feel the lights approaching her. Just in time she jumped into the trees as the heavy trucks passed by. There were two black cars, like the one Agent Kendall drove, and two trucks full of soldiers. She caught her breath when she saw that—she hadn't been expecting this at all. How had they found them? How had they known they were there? Maybe they had put some kind of device on her car, something that told them where she was going. Maybe they had seen that she wasn't going to Rochester after all. There was no use worrying about it now, she supposed. *Go home*, she said to herself. *This is the kind of trouble you don't get out of.* Instead she hurried on toward the gate.

Two agents she didn't know got out of the front car and started speaking to the men from the quarry standing at the gate. She didn't stay to listen to what they were saying, instead she moved quietly along the edge of the trees, trying to follow Lael. Soon she found a place where she could get inside. There were some metal buildings in front of her, and she stayed low to the ground as she went around behind them, running quickly across the gaps between each one. Eventually, she came to the end of the buildings and could see into the main quarry. There was a deep hole—the pit—in front of her, and she could see the moonlight on the water at the bottom of it. Behind it was the main rock face and over at the far side was a little purple light she knew must be Lael. She could tell the

guards at the gate wouldn't be able to see him, but if soldiers came into the grounds it wouldn't take long to find him. She had to warn him quickly. Should she go around the edge, taking longer and staying out of the light? Or should she run across and hope nobody saw her? Going around the edge was dangerous—she could easily fall into the water if the ground was loose—and she didn't have much time, so she made her decision. Holding her breath, she ran out from behind the building.

It wasn't more than twenty meters but it seemed like forever. Every moment she expected someone to shout out, to see her, but nobody did. By the time she got to the buildings at the other side, she was breathing hard. She guessed the last time she ran like that was at school. Lael was sitting on the ground. In front of him a small purple ring turned slowly in the air, and behind it the air was moving, just like it had moved when Lael had changed shape. But behind that, it was like the face of the quartz was running like water, no, like sand. It was breaking into little pieces with a *whooshing* sound and being pulled into the ring in front of Lael. This close, she was surprised at how loud it was—she was sure the guards would hear it soon and come running.

"It's working perfectly," Lael said. "My device is breaking down the quartz and sending it to my ship, which will . . ."

"Lael," Beth said, "we don't have time. There are soldiers. At the gate. They're coming. They're coming this way."

"Soldiers?" Lael said.

"And agents. The government agents."

"I can't go yet," Lael said. "I need a little longer. Only another minute or so."

Beth heard a noise behind her and went to the edge of a building to look around. There were maybe ten or fifteen soldiers coming into the quarry, spreading out and searching, their lights flicking out in front of them. Beth jumped behind the building before one of them saw her.

"Lael," she said, "they're here!"

"Beth, I can't," he said. "Even if I want to I can't. I can only do this once. If this doesn't work, I won't be going anywhere."

It's up to you, Beth found herself thinking. *Do something.* She saw an old bottle lying on the ground and it gave her an idea. She picked it up and then began to take off her jacket.

"What are you doing?" Lael asked.

She pulled down her T-shirt so one of her shoulders was bare and then walked out from behind the building. Holding the bottle out in front of her, she started to sing.

A light moved in her direction. Someone shouted, "Who is that?"

"Hey, boys!" said Beth. "What's going on?"

"Ma'am, identify yourself now!" a soldier shouted.

"She looks like she's had a few drinks to me," another said. "Is she an employee?"

"I don't know her," said another voice. This one sounded different, softer. Beth guessed it was a guard. "What are you doing here, ma'am?"

"We're having ourselves a party!" Beth said. "Come and join us."

"Get her out of here," someone shouted.

"Wait a minute," said a woman. Beth recognized the voice as Agent Kendall's and fear rose in her chest.

"Men, this woman is a target," Agent Kendall said. "Shoot her."

Beth froze and several things happened at once. As the soldiers came forward she felt movement behind her and then a thought in her mind, a *blue* thought which was as loud and as clear as any voice she'd ever heard: *Beth*, it said. *Close your eyes!*

She shut her eyes and threw her hands over her face. Then she screamed as the world behind them exploded with light.

Chapter 8

Departures

It wasn't only Beth—everyone was screaming. After a few moments she opened her eyes again. Agents Kendall and Stone were both lying on the ground, holding their faces and crying out. Some of the other soldiers were lying on the ground, others stood with their hands over their eyes shouting at each other for help. There was a pain behind Beth's eyes, but apart from that she was fine. What had just happened?

She felt a hand on her shoulder and turned around. It was Lael. He was covered in sweat and looked very tired. *He looks almost human,* Beth thought to herself. He started to fall and Beth had to help him.

"Please," he said, "could you help me?"

"What did you just do?" Beth asked. "Did you just do that?"

"I don't have much time," he said.

"What did you do to them?" Beth said.

"Don't worry," Lael said. "They'll be fine. Their eyes will be fine."

"Who's out there?" Agent Kendall shouted. "Where are we? What's going on?"

"Please," Lael said.

Still unsure what had just happened, Beth half-walked, half-carried Lael back to the car. They passed some more soldiers, but all of them were still holding their faces and they didn't stop them. When she got them back to the car, she didn't start it right away.

"What's wrong?" Lael said. "We must get back quickly."

"Tell me what you did!" Beth said. "If you hurt those people . . ."

"No, no. I couldn't do that. It's hard to explain," Lael said. He looked as if he was in pain.

"Agent Kendall didn't know where she was," Beth said. "What was that all about?"

"The . . . effect has confused them," Lael said. "But they will be back to normal soon. Mostly. Come on, Beth. Please."

"Promise me you didn't hurt them," Beth said.

"I promise," said Lael. "Please, before they come after us."

Back at the quarry, one or two of the soldiers had appeared at the gate. Beth could see them moving around slowly. It looked like Lael was telling the truth. Without starting the engine, she ran the car down to the road without any lights on. Then she started it up and drove slowly over the hill. When she was sure nobody at the quarry could see her, she switched on the car's lights and drove back to Beresford as fast as she could.

A few times some army trucks passed her, and she wondered how long it would be before cars appeared behind her, and what would happen when they were caught. When *she* was caught. What did the government do to people who helped aliens escape their own agents? She didn't know, but she guessed it wasn't anything good. She was thinking about all this as she approached her home and suddenly found herself stopping hard. Up ahead of them was a line of cars and trucks across the road. She couldn't go that way.

She switched off the lights and pulled onto the side of the road. Had anyone seen her? If they had, nobody was coming. Lael had his eyes closed as if he was sleeping. She shook his shoulder.

"What is it?" he said. "Are we at your home?"

"Look," Beth said. "Now what do we do?"

"How far is it to your place?"

"No more than five or six miles," said Beth. "About ten minutes' drive."

"Can we walk?" Lael asked.

"We could but . . . you don't look good, Lael."

"I will be fine," he said, getting out of the car.

"Change," she said. "Into . . . crystal. I'll carry you."

"I can't," he said. "I can't use my energy for that. I'll need all I have left."

The two of them climbed over the edge of the road into a field. Beth thought they could cut straight across to her house without following the road. For about an hour they walked, slowly, with Beth helping Lael. A few times he tripped and fell and she had to help him up. Her T-shirt was wet with sweat. She was so very tired.

"How far now?" Lael asked.

There was still a long way to go—they weren't even halfway. She was going to say "not far" but Lael had already picked the thought from her mind.

"That's enough," he said, lowering himself to the ground. "I can't go any farther."

"But we need to get to your ship," Beth said.

"We might be close enough," he replied.

He lifted up his hand and Beth saw he was still holding the ring, the one he had used up at the quarry. There was a blue-purple light in it, hard to see at first but getting brighter all the time. He was bent almost double—whatever he was doing was clearly hurting him. His body started shaking and his mouth fell open.

"Lael," Beth said. "Please, Lael, what's happening?"

Before he could reply, the light suddenly went out and Lael fell backwards onto the ground.

"Are you all right?" Beth asked, holding his arms. "What happened?"

"Over there," Lael said, his voice quiet. "The woods. Look. Now."

Beth looked. All she could see was the same field of stars she saw out of her window every night. She was about to say that to Lael, but then something stopped her. She couldn't be sure but it looked like there was a light in the distance.

"Something," Beth said. "A light."

She was wondering what it was, but then the point of light rose up in the sky like another star and started growing fast. Beth was scared for a moment until she realized what it was: Lael's ship coming toward them.

"It's here," he said, and seconds later it was. Lael had stood up too and was now looking at her.

"It's time for me to go," he said. Beth nodded. She found it hard to say anything. *So fast,* Beth thought. *Everything is happening so fast.*

"Wait," she said. "Before you go I want to say something. Thank you. For what you've shown me. Thank you so much." It was then that she started to cry. He put his arms around her.

"You can come with me, Beth," he said, quietly.

"Come with you?" She hadn't expected that. "Why? I mean why are you asking me?"

"Because you want to."

"I can't," Beth said. "I *don't* want to."

"Listen to me," Lael replied. He held both of her hands and looked deep into her eyes. "I know how life is for you here. You are unhappy. You are lonely."

"Don't say that. You don't . . ."

"You wish every day to go away, to live for yourself, to see the world. I can show you the universe. Your life is short. Make the most of it!"

"You don't have to give me anything, Lael."

"It's not only that. You know that. There is a connection between us. I have never experienced this before. It's a human thing, isn't it?"

Beth nodded. She could have told him what it was called, too.

"Come with me," he said. "We don't have much time."

She wanted to. She wanted to with all her heart, but she knew she could not because she had another connection, and he was waiting back at her house for her. That feeling of needing to get away—it was nothing compared to how much her father needed her.

"I see," Lael said, reading her thoughts. "I understand."

"I'm sorry," Beth said. She was crying now. Lael put his hand to her face and felt her tears.

"I understand," he said again and put his arms around her. She held him tightly in return. He was a man from another world but it felt like the most normal thing she had ever done.

"I will try to come back for you," Lael said. "I don't know if I can, but I will try."

"It's OK," Beth said. "Oh, they're getting so close."

They were, too. There were two helicopters coming toward them.

"Be strong," Lael said.

"I will," she replied. "Don't forget me."

"I won't. And I have left you a gift," Lael said, strangely. "Something to remember me by."

She wanted to ask him what he meant but knew he would not answer, so she just held him one last time. Her eyes were closed but she could feel a great light behind them. After it, there was nothing in her arms but air.

Lael and his ship were gone, and Beth stood alone in the open field.

Chapter 9

The gift

Beth was still standing there when the helicopters landed and the soldiers climbed out. There were also some agents, some men in suits and ties. They shouted at her, told her to get down, told her to get up, and then took her away in the helicopter. Beth said nothing—she didn't get the chance.

They flew for an hour or so. Beth didn't know where they went because they put a cloth over her face so she couldn't see anything. She was pleased about that; it meant nobody could see what she was going through. She felt lost without Lael, but she knew she'd have to calm herself down to get out of there. She started to make a plan. It was a good plan, she thought, and if she was lucky it might even get her home.

When they landed, two soldiers took her into a small office with no windows. She waited. Some time later, a soldier came in with a cup of coffee. Beth asked why she was there, why they were keeping her in that room, but the soldier didn't reply. Soon enough two agents appeared, a man and a woman just like Kendall and Stone. *I guess that's the way they do things around here*, Beth thought. *In pairs.*

"My name is Agent Parris," said the woman. "This is Agent Cline."

"Why am I here?" Beth asked. She forced some tears. "What have I done? What's happening to me?"

"Miss Fowler, I believe you can tell us more about that than anybody."

"I don't understand. I don't understand what's happening." She thought about Lael, wanting to make herself cry, and felt tears run down her face.

"Miss Fowler, please be calm," Parris said. "You must have been through a lot, but it's over now. We need your help to . . ."

"Don't you understand?" Beth shouted. "I don't know what's happened. I can't remember anything!"

"Sorry, Miss Fowler, you can't remember anything about what?"

"About anything! One minute I was at home with my Daddy, the next I'm standing out in a field, and you guys are telling me to get on the ground. What's happening?"

She bent over, crying hard while the agents whispered to each other. Beth knew they hadn't expected this. If she could convince them that she couldn't remember what happened, she knew there was a chance of getting home. The danger was Agent Kendall and Agent Stone. How long before they arrived and came in to see her? She knew they wouldn't believe her so easily.

"Miss Fowler, please be calm," Agent Parris said.

"Don't tell me to be calm," Beth said, standing up. "I feel like I'm losing my mind!"

She threw her hands over her face and started to cry again. This went on for some time. After a while she settled down and let them ask her a few questions, then got upset again and told them she couldn't remember a thing, that she needed to go home and take care of her Daddy. They seemed to believe her, and Beth found herself thinking they were going to let her go when the door opened and Agent Kendall and Agent Stone came in the room.

"Is this her?" Agent Parris asked them.

Beth prepared herself for the worst. Both of the agents studied her face for a moment.

They don't know me, Beth thought. *They can't remember who I am. How?* she started to ask herself, then remembered the light at the quarry and knew Lael had done it.

"I can't be sure," Kendall said.

"What about you?" Parris asked Stone. Stone shook his head.

"What a mess," Agent Parris said.

◇◇◇

They didn't keep her long after that. Before they sent her home they made her promise to see one of their doctors every week. They also made her sign a piece of paper saying she could never speak about it to anybody. Beth was happy to agree to it; she didn't want to tell anybody anything.

It was early morning when she got back and went in to see her father. He was lying in bed as always and she felt suddenly sick when she saw him. It was like she expected, somehow, that after everything had happened, things couldn't just go back to normal. For all this to happen only to be back to where she was . . . her head felt light and she fell onto her father's bed.

"Beth?" said a voice. *"Are you all right?"*

It was her father's.

"Daddy?" Beth said. "Did you just say something?"

"I did," he said again, but not by speaking. He was inside her mind. *"It seems as though that friend of yours has taught me his trick."*

"But how . . . how can you do this?" Beth asked.

"I just tried it when we were together before. I think your friend . . . Lael . . . I think he made a connection between us. Or maybe it was because we had a connection before."

"Oh, my," was all Beth said. "Oh my oh my."

"Why don't you try it?" said her father's voice.

No way, Beth thought. *I can't do that.*

"Sure you can," her father replied. Beth laughed in astonishment.

"I have left a gift," Lael had said, *"something to remember me by."* Now she knew what he meant. She put her arms around her father. Would Lael come back? She didn't know. Would the connection with her father last? She didn't know that. You never know what's going to happen tomorrow.

"But whatever it is, it's going to be all right," said her father. *"We're going to be all right."*

Review: Chapters 1–5

A. Number these events in the order they happened (1–6).

_____ Lael falls down outside Beth's house.

_____ Lael turns into a small purple crystal.

_____ Beth wakes up in the middle of the night.

_____ Some government agents arrive at Beth's house looking for Lael.

_____ Lael meets Beth's father.

_____ Lael realizes his ship is badly damaged.

B. Choose the best answer for each question.

1. Why does Beth get such a shock when she sees Lael outside her house?

a. Because Lael is an alien.

b. Because Lael isn't wearing any clothes.

c. Because it's the middle of the night.

2. Why doesn't Beth take Lael to the hospital when he collapses?

a. Because her car has run out of fuel.

b. Because she thinks he'll be all right.

c. Because she can't get him into the car.

3. Why does Beth NOT tell the government agents about Lael?

a. Because she wants to know how he knows about her.

b. Because she's fallen in love with him.

c. Because she doesn't like the government.

4. Why does Lael become a purple crystal?

    a. Because he wants Beth to believe him.

    b. Because it's his favorite trick and he wants to impress her.

    c. Because he wants to communicate with her clearly.

5. Why does Beth take a hammer with her to the forest?

    a. So she can repair Lael's ship.

    b. Because she doesn't fully trust Lael.

    c. Because she carries a hammer everywhere.

6. Why does Lael want to go to the quarry?

    a. Because it has quartz that he can use to repair his ship.

    b. Because it's a local sightseeing spot and he wants to see it.

    c. Because he thinks the government agents won't find him there.

7. Why can't Lael help Noel's illness?

    a. Because he doesn't know how.

    b. Because it would use too much power.

    c. Because he feels it would be wrong.

8. Why is Noel scared when he meets Lael?

    a. Because he doesn't like strange men in the house.

    b. Because he thinks Beth is in some kind of trouble.

    c. Because he can feel Lael inside his mind.

C. Complete each sentence using the correct word from the box.

alien	clearing	device	explode	hammer
multiple sclerosis	helicopter	repair	tricks	planets

1. A phone is a/an _____ for talking to someone in another place.

2. "Have you seen the movie *E.T.*? It's about a/an _____ who comes to visit Earth."

3. Flying in a/an _____ is extremely noisy.

4. Paul's computer isn't working so he's looking for someone to _____ it.

5. Hopefully, doctors will find a cure for _____ one day.

6. When you're walking in the woods, a/an _____ can be a nice place to sit and have a rest.

7. If you need to do repairs around the house, a/an _____ is very useful.

8. "Be careful—it looks like the bomb is about to _____!"

9. There are eight _____ in our solar system.

10. Magicians are people who are very good at performing _____.

Review: Chapters 6–9

A. Read each statement and circle whether it is true (T) or false (F).

1. Agents Kendall and Stone want to know what's in Beth's   T / F
   bag as she leaves the house.

2. Lael likes the feeling of being inside human minds.   T / F

3. Beth starts singing to keep the soldiers away from Lael.   T / F

4. Beth and Lael start walking because there are soldiers on   T / F
   the road.

5. Lael kills several of the soldiers.   T / F

6. Lael asks Beth to go in his ship with him.   T / F

7. Beth decides to go with Lael.   T / F

8. Lael leaves Beth his ring as a gift.   T / F

B. Complete each sentence using the correct word from the box.

Beth	Lael	Noel	Agent Kendall	Agent Parris

1. _____ doesn't know anything about Lael.

2. _____ pretends not to remember anything about Lael.

3. _____ doesn't remember anything about Lael.

4. _____ is the first to realize Lael has given them a gift.

5. _____ doesn't know if he will ever return.

C. Complete the crossword puzzle using the clues below.

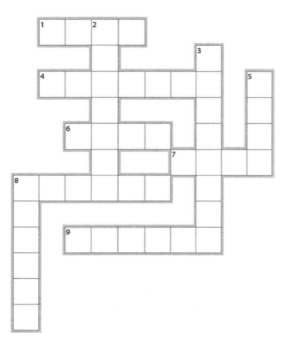

Across

1. an untidy situation
4. Lael's ship is made of this chemical element.
6. Give this to someone on their birthday.
7. When you bow to someone, you _____ at the waist.
8. You find stone here; rhymes with "sorry."
9. Without this, your car won't go very far.

Down

2. a person who fights for his or her country
3. You probably can't imagine anything as big as this.
5. If you go to a beach, you can try and count how many grains of these there are.
8. a type of silicon crystal which you sometimes find in watches

Answer Key

Chapters 1–5

A:

2, 4, 1, 3, 6, 5

B:

1. b; **2.** c; **3.** a; **4.** a; **5.** b; **6.** a; **7.** a; **8.** c

C:

1. device; **2.** alien; **3.** helicopter; **4.** repair; **5.** multiple sclerosis; **6.** clearing; **7.** hammer; **8.** explode; **9.** planets; **10.** tricks

Chapters 6–9

A:

1. F; **2.** T; **3.** T; **4.** T; **5.** F; **6.** T; **7.** F; **8.** F

B:

1. Agent Parris; **2.** Beth; **3.** Agent Kendall; **4.** Noel; **5.** Lael

C:

Across:

1. mess; **4.** silicon; **6.** gift; **7.** bend; **8.** quarry; **9.** engine

Down:

2. soldier; **3.** universe; **5.** sand; **8.** quartz

Background Reading:

Spotlight on . . . *Are we alone in the universe?*

Are we alone in the universe? Or is there other intelligent life out in the stars, perhaps watching us at this very moment? If you are like most people, you have probably thought about these questions at some time or other. Maybe you believe highly intelligent alien beings have visited our planet many times, helping us develop technology and science. Or maybe you believe, and some people do, that aliens sometimes come and take us away in their spaceships, to do scientific experiments on us, or put us in zoos. It's possible you believe that there is nobody else out there at all, and that human beings are one of a kind, all alone in the cold darkness of space.

A very specific set of conditions were required to create life like we have on Earth, almost like a recipe. First you need a certain kind of sun, of a certain size and age. Just like our Sun, in fact. Next you need a certain kind of planet, made of certain kinds of materials. This planet can't be too hot or too cold, and it must have the right kind of gravity, so it must be a certain distance from the sun, just like ours is. Once you have the right kind of sun and the right kind of planet at the right distance, then you need time.

Life doesn't develop instantly—it needs lots of time, and intelligent life needs even more time to learn and become intelligent. Our own species has taken over half a million years or so to reach this point of development (the point where we have just started sending things into space), which is actually very short when you compare it to a lot of other species. Still, a lot of things can happen in two million years. If, for example, Earth had been struck by a large meteor sometime during this time, we would probably all have been killed. This is what scientists believe happened to the dinosaurs—if it hadn't, maybe they would be sending ships into outer space, too!

Think About It

1. Do you think intelligent life exists outside our planet Earth?
2. If alien beings visited us one day, what would you ask them about their world?

Glossary

alien	(*n.*)	a creature from outer space
clearing	(*n.*)	a piece of land, as in a forest, that contains no trees or bushes
device	(*n.*)	a thing made for a particular purpose, usually mechanical or electrical
engine	(*n.*)	part of a car or other vehicle that makes it move
explode	(*v.*)	burst, fly into pieces, or break up violently with a loud noise
gift	(*n.*)	a special ability or talent; something you give to someone as a present
hammer	(*n.*)	a tool used for hitting nails
helicopter	(*n.*)	a kind of aircraft with rotating wings or blades
mess	(*n.*)	something that is untidy or dirty
multiple sclerosis	(*n.*)	a serious disease of the central nervous system. People who have it often find it difficult to walk and speak.
quarry	(*n.*)	a pit or mine, usually open to the air, from which stone or other material is obtained by cutting, blasting, etc.
quartz	(*n.*)	one of the most common minerals, silicon dioxide (SiO_2)
sand	(*n.*)	the fine debris of rocks, consisting of small, loose grains, often of quartz
silicon	(*n.*)	a non-metallic element (Si). A quarter of the Earth's crust is made of it.
trick	(*n., v.*)	something designed to deceive someone
universe	(*n.*)	all of the objects throughout space; the cosmos